What Lives In The Garden?

John Woodward

GARETH**STEVENS**
GS
PUBLISHING
A Member of the WRC Media Family of Companies

Please visit our web site at: www.garethstevens.com
For a free color catalog describing Gareth Stevens Publishing's list of high-quality books
and multimedia programs, call 1-800-542-2595 (USA) or 1-800-387-3178 (Canada).
Gareth Stevens Publishing's fax: (414) 332-3567.

Library of Congress Cataloging-in-Publication Data

Woodward, John, 1954-
  What lives in the garden? / John Woodward. — North American ed.
     p. cm. — (What lives in...?)
  Includes index.
   ISBN-13: 978-0-8368-7859-2 (lib. bdg.)
  1. Garden animals—Juvenile literature. [1. Garden animals. 2. Insects.
3. Arthropods. 4. Animals.] I. Title.
QL119.W66   2007
591.75'54—dc22   2006035783

This North American edition first published in 2007 by
Gareth Stevens Publishing
A Member of the WRC Media Family of Companies
330 West Olive Street, Suite 100
Milwaukee, WI 53212 USA

This U.S. edition copyright © 2007 by Gareth Stevens, Inc.
Original edition copyright © 2000 by Haldane Mason Ltd.
First published in 2000 by Red Kite Books, an imprint of
Haldane Mason Ltd., P.O. Box 34196, London NW10 3YB, United Kingdom.
(info@haldanemason.com)

Editors: Beck Ward and Ben Keith
Art director: Jonathan Hair
Designer: Phil Ford

Gareth Stevens editor: Leifa Butrick
Gareth Stevens art direction: Tammy West
Gareth Stevens graphic designer: Charlie Dahl

Photo credits: (t=top, b=bottom, l=left, r=right, c=center)
Bruce Coleman Collection: /M.P.L. Fogden 11; /Jen & Des Bartlett 25t; /Jon Cancalosi 25b; Holt Studios International: /Nigel Cattlin 39t;
Natural History Museum: 12; NHPA: /N. Callow 8b, 14, 17t, 26, 40t; /Martin Garwood 15t, 16t 21t; /Martin Wendler 21b; /G.I. Bernard 22; /
A.N.T. 24l; /Richard Knightbridge 30; /Dr Eckart Pott 38; /Daniel Heuclin 33; /Stephen Dalton 7b, 10r, 17b 20b, 24b; /Dan Griggs 39;
Oxford Scientific Films: /Jorge Sierra 8t; /Mantis Wildlife Films 16b, 40b; /G.A. Maclean 18; /John Cheverton 31t; /David G. Fox 20t; /
Jim Bockowski 41t; /Breck P. Kent 41b; Premaphotos Wildlife: /Ken Preston-Mafham 24t; Science Photo Library: /Andrew Syred 6, 29,
32; /Eye of Science 4, 42; /Claude Nuridsany & Marie Perennou 5, 7t, 10l, 13b, 23, 28, 35-7; /Dr Jeremy Burgess 9, 15b, 31b, 43t; /Dr John
Brackenbury 13t; /Simone D. Pollard 27t; /Sinclair Stammers 34; /David Scharf 19; /Dr Morley Read 43b.

Printed in Canada

1 2 3 4 5 6 7 8 9 10 10 09 08 07 06

Contents

Introduction

Some of the most fascinating animals in the world live just a few steps from your back door. You do not have to go to the African plains or the Amazon rain forests to see them. Just step outside and take a walk down your garden path.

If it is summer, the place will be full of sounds — bees buzzing on the flowers, grasshoppers chirping in the grass, and hoverflies humming through the air.

This orb web spider waits patiently for its insect prey.

It's a Jungle Out There!

Once you start looking, you will discover more and more little animals. You will see spiders building their wonderful webs or sneaking up on their victims. You will see ants taking care of flocks of aphids and nasty-looking insects crawling from the pond and turning themselves into jeweled dragonflies. It is magical!

A garden is a like a miniature, or small-scale, nature reserve for tiny creatures. You may find a few bigger animals in it as well, such as mice and rabbits, but they like to stay hidden. Insects and their leggy friends — and enemies — are not so shy. They go on with their lives whether you are there or not. It is great to watch them. And who knows? They may be watching you, too!

Untidy Paradise

Some gardens are better for small animals than others. Big, old gardens that have gone wild are best because they provide many places to live and plants to feed on. Most gardens are not wild, of course, but they do sometimes have wild corners, handy heaps of dead leaves, or comfortable piles of logs for small creatures to live in.

Blackflies like to suck blood — so beware!

Killer Spray

Some garden animals are pests. They eat the plants, and some may bite or sting. A few animals may even be dangerous. Many people think that the garden is better off without them, and they spray poisonous chemicals on the plants, hoping to kill these tiny creatures. Sometimes it works, but then more pests usually come along. The plants have to be sprayed again, and the poison kills all the other small creatures as well, including the ones that eat the pests. Eventually, most of the insects disappear, along with the spiders and birds that prey upon them, and the garden is just not the same.

What Lives in the Grass?

Most gardens have a patch of grass or even a prize-winning lawn that looks and feels like a green carpet. Many gardens, however, are bumpy playgrounds full of bikes and barbecue grills. In the city, they are usually next to other gardens, but out of town, the grass is often an extension of a half-wild meadow, railroad embankment, or roadside. If they get the chance, the creatures that live out on the rough grassland will slip through the fence and move into your garden. Often these newcomers do not get much of a chance to settle down and build homes because someone mows the lawn once a week or so. In areas beneath trees and fences, however, the grass can grow tall, forming a miniature jungle and offering food and shelter to all kinds of climbing and burrowing insects — and to the spiders and other killers that eat them.

Songs of Summer

What would summer be without grasshoppers? These noisy insects love wide stretches of long grass, where they use their tough biting jaws to eat the grass blades. Male grasshoppers make their chirpy songs by rubbing a row of pegs on the inside of each long back leg against the tough edge of a folded wing. Some females can sing too, but not as loud.

Male grasshoppers sing to attract females.

High Jumpers

If you get too close to a grasshopper, it will fall silent and leap away, shooting itself into the air with its power-packed hind legs. Many grasshoppers can also fly, by suddenly opening a set of dazzlingly bright hind wings. When they land, they hide their colored wings and disappear, like sparks going out. It is a clever way of confusing their enemies, and it certainly confuses us!

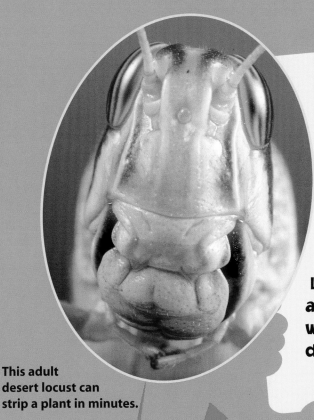

Locust Plague

The locusts that live in desert areas are really just big grasshoppers. If rain turns their desert into a green garden, they multiply so fast that they eat every plant in the area. They fly off in search of more food — in huge swarms of up to fifty billion insects. Locusts can land on unguarded fields and eat all the crops on a whole farm within hours. A big swarm can even destroy a whole country's food supply.

This adult desert locust can strip a plant in minutes.

Megaphone

The grasshopper's song is just a scratchy buzz, but some crickets make really musical sounds. The field cricket is a shiny black beast that sings near the entrance to its burrow down among the grass. The champion singer is the muscular, burrowing mole cricket. It digs a trumpet-shaped burrow that acts like a megaphone and makes its song louder. On summer evenings, you can hear its deep, soft churr for more than 1 mile (2 kilometers) away.

The strong back legs of a grasshopper are designed for a fast getaway.

Eerie Glow

While some insects sing to attract mates, others glow. Long grass sometimes contains female glowworms that climb the stems at dusk to flash their valentine messages into the summer night. Each glowworm is a wingless beetle with light organs in her tail. These glow with an eerie, yellow-green light when oxygen combines with a protein called luciferin and an enzyme called luciferase. The light organs are connected to special air tubes to make sure they get a good oxygen supply. By opening and closing the tubes, a glowworm can turn herself on and off.

Glowworms are like night-lights for other animals!

BUG ALERT!

Flashpoints

- a glowworm's chemical lamp is not wasteful; 98 percent of the energy is turned into light, not heat — luckily for the glow-worm!
- Young glowworms are hungry predators that attack snails, injecting them with digestive juices that turn the snails' insides into soup.
- Fireflies can also produce light and flash coded messages at each other.

Furry Miners

A few insects live under the lawn. In spring, you may notice small holes appearing on bare patches, each surrounded by a volcanolike cone of soil grains. These are the burrows of mining bees. If you watch one of the holes, you may see its builder. She looks like a miniature bumblebee and always lives alone. She lays eggs in her burrow and supplies them with pellets of nectar and pollen gathered from flowers. Then she seals the hole and flies away.

Mining bees like to nest underground.

Busy Ants

Ants go everywhere in the garden, but some are particularly busy among the blades of grass. Energetic harvester ants, for example, gather the seeds of grasses and other garden plants and carry them back to their nests. They then store them in special underground rooms where they keep for many weeks. When the ants need food, they raid the seed store, just as we might raid the refrigerator.

This black ant defends itself by squirting a strong acid at an attacker.

Ant Wars

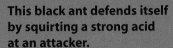

Occasionally, a harvester ant meets its deadly enemy — the fire ant. Fire ants live in huge colonies in southern United States. They are tiny, yet ferocious, with biting jaws and painful stings. They attack anything that threatens them — even people.

Fire ants often wipe out other types of ants living in the same area, so if a wandering harvester meets a fire ant, both rush back to their own nests to get soldiers to help. The ant armies meet and fight. War often becomes slaughter, and dead and dying ants litter the grass.

Secret Weapon

Ants also fight battles with termites. Most termites eat dead wood, but the harvester termites of the tropics feast on young grass shoots. Harvester termites busily hunt for food all around the nest and often get into gardens.

Millions of termites live together in a colony, looking after one breeding queen. "Worker" termites are easy prey for ants, so heavily armed soldier termites defend them. Soldier termites may have huge biting jaws or long snouts that squirt a sticky, irritating glue that gums up the attacking ants' jaws.

BUG ALERT!

Living Trap

Search in the long grass in any warm area, from New York to California, and you may discover a mean killer lurking there — the praying mantis. It is not easy to see because it makes itself look like a blade of grass to hide from its victims.

A mantis sits and waits, holding its barbed forelegs up as if praying. When an unsuspecting insect strays within range, the mantis watches it closely with its spooky eyes and then suddenly snatches the poor insect in a split-second strike. Impaled on the mantis' forelegs, the insect is helpless, and the mantis calmly eats it alive.

Money Pit

The purse web spider lives in a burrow with a lining that sticks up above ground, just like a silk purse. When an insect walks over the purse, the spider runs up and skewers it through the silk with its extralong fangs. It cuts a slit in the purse, pulls its victim inside, and sews up the hole.

Victims of the praying mantis do not feel blessed when they get speared by its forelegs.

Mantis Morsels

- A mantis can turn its head all the way around, to follow every move of an unsuspecting, approaching victim.
- If it catches a dangerous stinging insect, the praying mantis may kill it by biting off its head.
- The female praying mantis is notorious for eating the male during mating, often snacking on his head.

Is that grass moving or is it a grass spider?

Megamouth

When you look for a praying mantis, you may see a grass spider. It hides from enemies by stretching its front four legs forward in a bunch, pretending to be part of a grass stem. These spiders have huge jaws, and the male uses his to grip the female's fangs during mating to prevent her from eating him.

Big and Hairy

The spiders you see most often in the grass are wolf spiders — hunters that can run fast and chase their prey instead of trapping them in webs. Some wolf spiders sit in burrows and pounce on passing insects. These home lovers have a muscular European cousin with the scientific name *Lycosa tarantula*. It is the original tarantula that gave its name to the huge bird-eating spiders of South America. You might meet a desert tarantula in Arizona, New Mexico, or southern California. It is very different from the European wolf spider, however, with long hairy legs, enormous fangs, and tiny, virtually useless eyes.

Tarantula Tidbits

- American tarantulas can have a legspan of up to 5 inches (13 centimeters), but some of their relatives from the Amazon, like the Goliath bird-eating spider, have a legspan of up to 11 inches (28 cm)!
- These giant spiders really do eat birds, if they can catch them, as well as bats and frogs. Mostly, however, they eat big juicy insects such as beetles.
- American tarantulas are covered with fine hairs that break easily and stick in your skin like splinters.

BUG ALERT!

Tarantula Hawk

It is hard to imagine any insect winning a fight with a tarantula, but one insect in the Southwest specializes in hunting these monster spiders. It is called a tarantula hawk, but it is actually a big wasp with a serious sting. She tracks down a tarantula in its burrow and lures it out to fight. As the spider tries to stab the wasp with its fangs, the wasp slips under its guard and stabs it with her sting.

A huge hairy spider makes an easy victim for the giant tarantula hawk.

11

What Visits the Flowers?

Back in the nineteenth century, fearless plant hunters explored distant places on the planet in search of unique and unheard of flowers. They brought back thousands of different plants and seeds and, over the years, these were crossbred to create plants that never existed before. Most garden flowers were created in this way.

These plants look great, but they puzzle the wildlife. Their leaves taste all wrong, so most native plant-eating insects steer clear of them. This is good news for gardeners, but it means fewer caterpillars and other juicy grubs are around to attract songbirds. The sugary nectar in their flowers is fine, however, so adult insects fly in to refuel at exotic flowering plants like buddleias. Although long grass is home for many creatures, a flower garden is like a filling station for insects, where most visitors are just passing through.

Iridescent Scales

The most obvious nectar-feeding insects are butterflies. They live all over the world and dazzle us with their beauty. Their wonderful wings are big transparent plates made of a plasticlike material called chitin and covered with tiny colored scales arranged like the tiles on a roof. As butterflies get older, they lose these scales and gradually go bald!

Some wing scales reflect light in iridescent blues and purples. Other scales give off fragrances that a possible mate cannot resist. This perfume is important because some butterflies only live for a few weeks — just long enough to mate and lay their eggs.

Butterflies like this tortoiseshell are often more colorful than the flowers they visit.

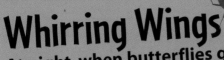

Whirring Wings

At night, when butterflies go to bed, moths come out. They are attracted to plants like honeysuckle that become more fragrant at night. Fewer flowers are open at night, so the insects go straight from one plant to another.

Butterflies and moths are similar, but they have different ways of flying . While butterflies flap their wings, moths beat them at high speed. This method enables moths to hover like hummingbirds. One type of moth is actually called the hummingbird hawk moth. Unlike most moths, it flies by day, so you can marvel at it hovering over a flower, inserting its long tongue to drink.

Moths don't get in a flap. They whirr their wings!

Hover Power

Seeming to float nearby may be an insect that looks like a bundle of golden-brown fur with a long pin sticking out in front. It is a bee fly. It does not really hover, or float, however. It clings to a flower with its feet while it drinks with its long proboscis.

The bee fly is amusing, but it has a dark secret. It lays its eggs near the nests of mining bees and, when they hatch, the bee fly maggots crawl into the nests, find the young bees growing inside, and slowly eat them alive.

Big mouth strikes again! The bee fly drinks nectar through its long, tubular tongue.

Pollen Baskets

The busiest nectar feeders in the flower garden are the honeybees, and with good reason. They live in colonies of fifty thousand or more, and all the food for the colony is collected by about half the worker bees. They must feed their queen, the other workers, and all the young bee grubs, too.

Nectar is mostly sugar, so to give the growing young a balanced diet, the bees also gather protein-rich pollen. The foraging worker bees carry the pollen back to the hive in pollen baskets on their hind legs. At the hive, they give the pollen and nectar to other bees. These turn the nectar into honey and then store it with the pollen in wax honeycomb cells to feed the colony throughout the winter. It is up to the workers to keep the hive going. No wonder they are so busy!

Bee Business

- When a honeybee finds a good source of nectar, she returns to the hive and lets the other bees know by doing a special dance called a waggle dance. The dance tells them how good the nectar is, which way to go, and how far away it is.
- All worker bees in a colony are sisters. They are the daughters of a single breeding female, the queen, but they cannot lay eggs. They have a few brothers, called drones, but not many. The workers do all the work, including raising a few females that will eventually become queens, too.

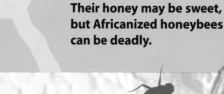

Their honey may be sweet, but Africanized honeybees can be deadly.

Killer Bees

In Latin America, most of the honey-bees have interbred with imported African bees. They are much more fierce than normal bees and, if anyone goes too close to their nests, they attack in swarms. Many people die from these attacks every year, so they are known as killer bees. They make excellent honey, however.

Furry Heavyweights

The most spectacular bees in the garden are big, furry bumblebees. They, too, live in colonies, with many worker bees that take care of a single queen, but their underground colonies are smaller and last for just one summer.

Bumblebees feed on nectar and pollen. They have long tongues so they can reach deep into flowers. Some flowers, such as lupins, are made just for bumblebees. They have special spring-loaded landing platforms. When a heavy bumblebee lands on the platform, the flower opens so the bee can get at the nectar. Since smaller, lighter insects cannot do this, the bumblebees know that lupins have probably not been raided already.

Hardworking bumblebees never take a day off.

Death Grip

Sometimes a bee or a butterfly seems to be sitting strangely still on a flower. If you look more closely, you will see it is stone dead, impaled on the fangs of a spider with a wonderful disguise.

The killer is a crab spider. It moves sideways, just like a crab. The most common type is nearly always white, and it likes to sit on the white rays of a daisy, where it is practically invisible.

The spider's strategy is simple. It sits by a source of nectar and waits, with its front legs held open wide. If an insect settles for a drink, the spider grabs it and then stabs the struggling victim with its fangs, shooting a powerful poison that kills it within seconds. Then, the spider pumps digestive juices into the dead body to liquefy its flesh and sucks it dry.

A hopeful white crab spider tries its luck on a pink flower.

Open House

While some flowers are shaped to attract certain insects, others are open to all. They are often alive with flies, bees, and small beetles such as rose chafers and soldier beetles, all feeding on the nectar and getting dusted with pollen.

Flowers also attract spider-hunting wasps, such as the tarantula hawks and ichneumon wasps, as well as other predators or parasites. Although these insects feed their young on the flesh of other animals, the adults prefer nectar.

Look closely into the flowers in your garden. This beautiful rose chafer is just one of the hidden delights.

Flowery Peril

The crab spider fools its victims because its color exactly matches that of the flower it is sitting on. Some tropical killers go even further and actually look like flowers. One of these is the orchid mantis, a relative of the praying mantis. It is often brightly colored, with parts of its body that look like the petals of an orchid.

The mantis perches motionless on a stem, its spiked arms held up, ready for action. If an insect lands on the plant, or even flies past, the mantis grabs it with a lightning movement and devours it.

An orchid mantis wears the ultimate disguise.

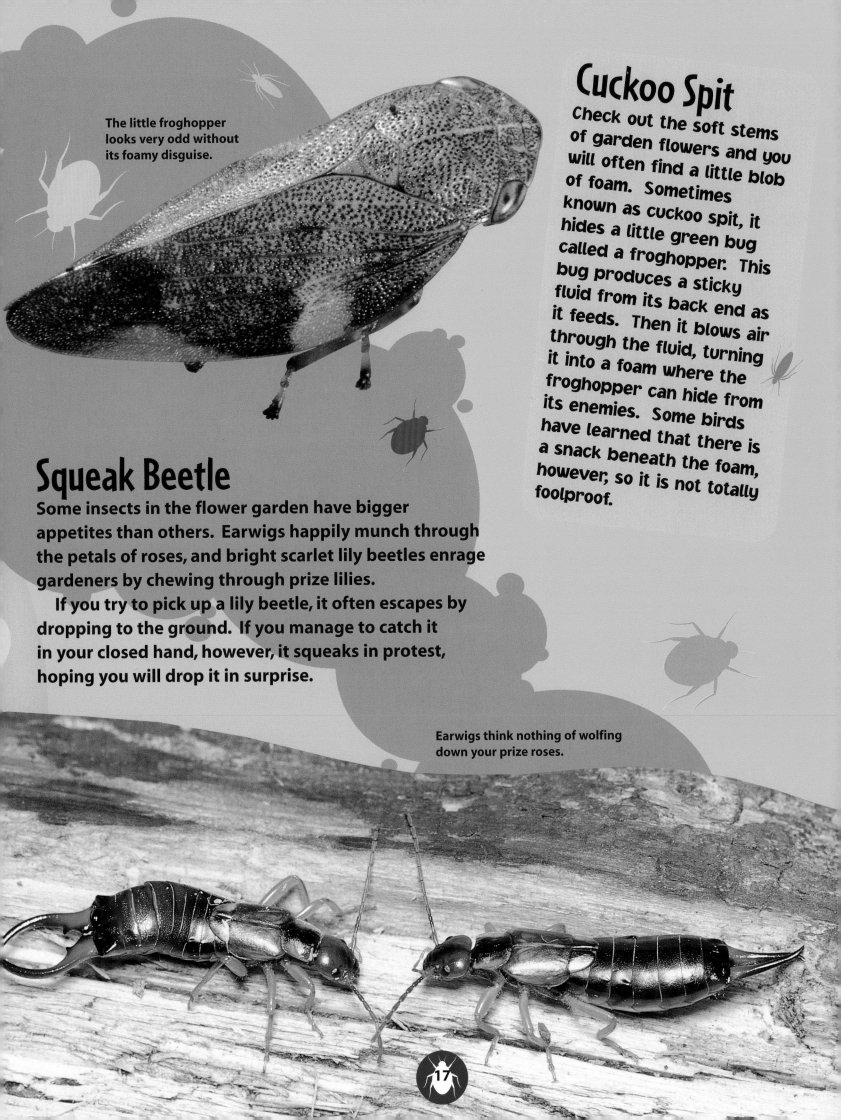

The little froghopper looks very odd without its foamy disguise.

Cuckoo Spit

Check out the soft stems of garden flowers and you will often find a little blob of foam. Sometimes known as cuckoo spit, it hides a little green bug called a froghopper. This bug produces a sticky fluid from its back end as it feeds. Then it blows air through the fluid, turning it into a foam where the froghopper can hide from its enemies. Some birds have learned that there is a snack beneath the foam, however, so it is not totally foolproof.

Squeak Beetle

Some insects in the flower garden have bigger appetites than others. Earwigs happily munch through the petals of roses, and bright scarlet lily beetles enrage gardeners by chewing through prize lilies.

If you try to pick up a lily beetle, it often escapes by dropping to the ground. If you manage to catch it in your closed hand, however, it squeaks in protest, hoping you will drop it in surprise.

Earwigs think nothing of wolfing down your prize roses.

What Buzzes around Your Head?

What could be nicer than lunch in the garden, among the flowers and birdsong? It always seems like a terrific idea, until insects join the feast. Some want to eat your food, like the gangs of stripy wasps that make people flap their hands wildly to shoo them away. Other bugs want to take a bite out of you, and you may not even notice until bumps appear on your skin the next day.

Striped Marauders

Any summer picnic attracts stripy, stinging wasps. Adult wasps serve chewed-up caterpillars to their queen's young, but they prefer something sweeter for themselves. A slice of cake or a juicy peach is a perfect treat. The fact that you might be trying to eat it does not bother them. Wave them away, and they just come back, time after time. If you actually hit one, don't be surprised if it stings you.

Just Admire

Some creatures that come buzzing around your head can look alarming but do not cause any trouble at all. They are hoverflies — nectar- and pollen-eating flies that often look just like wasps. Their stripes are a clever defensive trick, because birds are naturally wary of anything that looks as if it might sting.

When a hoverfly lands, you can see it is not a wasp. Its eyes are different, with huge honeycomb lenses like a blowfly. It also has only two wings instead of four, which improves its flying skill. It can fly forwards, backwards, and sideways. It can hover in exactly the same place and then fly away at such speed that you lose track of it. If it comes and hovers right in front of your face, don't panic — just admire.

The hoverfly may look like a wasp, but actually it is completely harmless.

Bloodsuckers

Wasps are annoying, but at least they are only after your lunch. The real villains are mosquitoes, midges, and blackflies. These are all two-winged flies, like hoverflies, but with much nastier habits. The females need to eat protein-rich food so they can lay eggs, and one of the richest foods of all is fresh blood.

Mosquitoes and midges are supplied with fine hypodermic needles. They slip them into your skin quite painlessly, and they can bite you several times before you notice. Blackflies, however, hack at you with their scissor jaws — and they do it in swarms! Swarms of blackflies have made some areas of the world almost uninhabitable.

Wasp Sandwich

If you are eating outdoors, make sure that any food you are about to bite into does not have a wasp on it. The wasp may sting you inside your mouth or throat. The sting then swells up, and besides being painful, can make it difficult or even impossible to breathe.

Nasty Diseases

Bloodsucking is bad enough, but insects also carry diseases. Tropical mosquitoes transmit malaria and yellow fever, which kill millions of people every year. Blackflies can carry an infection called river blindness, where thousands of tiny parasitic worms infest a person's skin and eyes. Together, these bloodsucking flies probably cause more misery than any other creature on Earth.

Blackflies are always on the lookout for the chance to steal some of your blood!

What Lives in the Bushes?

If you go out early on a summer morning, you will see the bushes decorated with spiders' webs, all silvery with morning dew. They look magical, but just think. Each one of those webs is a deadly trap. How do you think insects feel about spider webs? Imagine living in a city where there is a giant trap at the end of every street, occupied by a man-eating monster. Scary, huh?

That is not all. Assassins hide behind the leaves of every bush, and muggers lurk in the shadows. Some killers will lure a male insect to his doom by releasing a scent that imitates the perfume of a courting female. These hunters can only survive if they have plenty of victims, so a good crop of webs is a sign that the bushes are teeming with life.

The garden spider is almost blind, but it is still a killer.

Hedgeclipper

If you have a privet hedge around your garden, you may find an impressive green caterpillar with purple and white diagonal stripes devouring its leaves. The caterpillar of the privet hawk moth is a big moth that lays its eggs on the leaves of this bush. Although most butterflies and moths are choosy about where they lay their eggs, the privet hawk moth is lucky because its favorite food makes an excellent hedge. The hedge may not be quite so excellent after the caterpillars have been at it, however!

Low Profile

Most insects in the bushes try to make themselves hard to see, but the real masters of this art are stick insects and leaf insects. These amazing creatures are so well camouflaged that they look like part of the vegetation.

During the day, they stay very still, hoping to avoid hungry birds. They feed at night, moving very slowly. It is strange to see one leaf being eaten by another or a green shoot being devoured by a stick. It is good they don't try to eat each other!

Privet hawk moth caterpillars like to veg out on a good hedge.

Leaf-cutter Bee

You may see a small bee slicing neat oval sections out of rose leaves with her scissor jaws. Since bees drink nectar, what is a bee doing eating leaves?

Watch closely, and you will see that she does not eat them. She carries the leaf sections away to her burrow, rolls them into neat tubes, and stuffs each one with nectar and pollen. Then she lays an egg in the tube and seals it up. Eventually, she fills the burrow with these leaf cells. When they hatch, the grubs feed on the nectar and pollen, and emerge as adults the following year.

Leaf-cutter bees can spend all day cutting up plants for use in their burrows.

Evening Chorus

Bushes and shrubs often harbor handsome relatives of the grasshopper called bush crickets. Slow-moving and less likely to hop, they are often a beautiful emerald green with extralong antennae, or feelers. The female has a bladelike ovipositor on her tail that she uses for inserting eggs into small cracks and crevices. It looks alarming, but it is quite harmless.

Sticky Stuff
- Some stick insects breed without mating. The unfertilized eggs all hatch as females. After a while, males get very scarce and may even disappear.
- One Asian species of stick insect grows to 13 inches (33 cm), making it the world's longest insect.

BUG ALERT!

The wicked-looking sword on the tail of this bush cricket is simply for laying eggs.

Sapsuckers

Some insects live by sucking the sugary sap from the stems of plants. So-called "true bugs" have sharp, tubular mouthparts that they use like hypodermic needles. Greenflies and broad-bodied shield bugs are "true bugs," and many of them defend themselves with smelly fluids from special glands, so they are sometimes known as stink bugs.

The most extraordinary sapsuckers are the cicadas. In the warmer parts of the world, male cicadas fill the night air with chirping, buzzing, and whistling songs, which they produce using two thin plates on their sides called tymbals. By rattling the tymbals back and forth at high speed, the cicada produces a stream of clicks that sounds like a buzz or chirp.

Cicadas will sing whether you like it or not!

Assassins

Not all bugs are sapsuckers. Some are predators with big appetites, such as assassin bugs. They stalk through the leaves in search of prey. Some lurk in flowers waiting to ambush bees and other visitors.

When an assassin catches something, it uses its needle-sharp beak to stab it and inject paralyzing nerve poisons. These poisons mix with digestive juices that immediately start liquefying its victim's flesh inside its tough outer skin. The bug sucks the flesh through its beak as if it were drinking a milk shake with a straw. By the time it has finished slurping every last drop, its luckless victim is just an empty shell.

Cicada Data

- A cicada spends most of its life underground as a nymph. It sings only in the last few weeks of its life.
- Each cicada species has a different song so the male attracts the right female.
- The American periodical cicada stays in the ground for up to seventeen years. All the cicadas in a certain area emerge in the same year, lay their eggs and then vanish again.

Silken Snares

The most obvious killers in the bushes are the orb web spiders that weave their snares across the flyways of their insect prey. Each web is a spiral of sticky silk, with radial spokes of nonsticky silk. Often the spider sits at the center of its web, but if it feels a little exposed, it may seek shelter behind a nearby leaf, holding a single silk thread leading to the middle of the web.

At the slightest twitch, the orb web spider runs down the line, pauses to locate its prey, and then strikes. It works by touch alone because it is almost blind. When it reaches the struggling insect, the spider bites it to inject paralyzing venom, wraps it in thick silk, and settles down to dinner.

Running Jump

As an assassin bug sneaks around one side of a bush, a lynx spider patrols the other. Lynx spiders are hunters that leap on their prey like cats. They have good eyesight, and many species can pinpoint prey from a distance. They jump from leaf to leaf until they are close enough to pounce.

Some lynx spiders have emerald-green bodies, disguising them so well against leaves that they can just sit and wait. They are sure-footed enough to leap at flying insects (even dragonflies), lug them into the bushes, and kill them.

An *Argiope* spider weaves a cross to warn birds that might fly through its web.

Web Warning

The most spectacular orb web spiders are the big, striped, Argiope spiders found in warm countries. They weave zigzags of fluffy white silk in the middle of their webs, often in the pattern of a cross. Spiders that build their webs high up in bushes often add these crosses.

It seems that the white cross is a warning to birds. After all, if a bird flies into an Argiope web, the spider is left with a big repair job. The cross keeps the birds away, but for some reason, insect prey do not seem to notice it.

Stretch Wrap

Some spiders have come up with amazing ways of using silk to catch prey. The tropical gladiator spider, which uses its huge eyes to locate its victims at night, has one of the cleverest methods.

The gladiator's weapon is its net — a tiny web no bigger than a postage stamp, woven from elastic silk. The spider can grip the corners of the net in its front legs and stretch the net out wide. The gladiator suspends itself a few inches from the ground by a silken thread and hangs upside down, waiting for prey. When a victim appears, the spider suddenly extends all its legs at once, shoots down to stretch the net over its target, and snares the insect in a tangle of silk. Then, one quick shot of poison and it's all over.

A gladiator spider widens its net in hungry anticipation.

Fatal Attraction

When it comes to sneaky spider tricks, the prize must go to the bolas spider. This tropical hunter catches flying moths by grabbing them out of the night air with a ball of glue on the end of a silken thread. With one leg, the bolas spider whirls the ball around until it sticks to a moth. Then it pulls in its prey like a fish.

The really smart trick is the way the spider lures moths to its trap. It releases a chemical called a pheromone that smells like the scent that female moths release when they are ready to mate. Eager male moths are attracted from all over, and the spider simply waits until one flies by. How mean is that?

A bolas spider loves to fish for moths.

Stripy Snails

Bushes are often full of small snails with attractively banded shells. They feed near the ground but shelter in the bushes. There are two species. One has a white lip on its shell; the other has a brown lip. They vary so much in color that you could easily collect six or seven quite different empty shells in as many minutes.

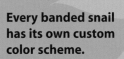

Every banded snail has its own custom color scheme.

Behind Closed Doors

Some of the most fascinating spiders hide underground. One of these is the trapdoor spider, which lives in the warmer parts of the world. Each spider builds a silk-lined tunnel with a hinged trapdoor at the entrance. The trapdoor fits like a cork in a bottle. During the day, the spider clings to the underside of the door, holding it shut against spider-hunting wasps. At night, however, it raises the door part way and peers out, waiting. When something edible wanders within range, the spider surges forward, stabs it with its poison fangs, and drags it back into the burrow. The door slams shut, and the spider can enjoy its meal in private.

Flip back the lid of a trapdoor spider's burrow, and you could get a nasty surprise.

Arachnofax

- One American bolas spider has the scientific name Mastophora dizzydeani, after the famous baseball player Jerome "Dizzy" Dean.
- The huge receptor cells in the gladiator spider's eyes can absorb two thousand times more light, per cell, than those of spiders that hunt during the day.
- A lynx spider can spray venom like a spitting cobra. If you find one, don't upset it!

One spit from this tiny lynx spider, and you could be feeling ill.

What Sits on the Wall?

An outdoor wall can attract all kinds of small creatures. Old walls are full of holes that make dry refuges for spiders, scorpions, wasps, bees, and lizards. Sunlit walls also warm up like storage heaters during the day, so they are ideal perches for animals that enjoy sunbathing.

Many flying insects rely on the sun's energy to keep them going, and they like to rest with their wings angled towards the sun like solar panels. When they have recharged their batteries, they take off and go about their business — provided the spiders, scorpions, and lizards do not get to them first.

Basking Flies

Flies are among the most cheerful sunbathers. Many are dull colored, but a few are dazzlingly beautiful. The iridescent, metallic sheen of a greenbottle, for example, is so marvelous that you can almost forget it was once a maggot munching dead flesh.

If you live near a farm, your wall may be visited by horseflies with astonishing patterns of green, red, and purple on their big compound eyes. These patterns are caused by the scattering of reflected light from the thousands of lenses in each eye. But watch out! These flies are bloodsuckers, and they might take a bite out of you.

The ruby-tailed cuckoo wasp has a stunning, colored body. It almost looks like a flying jewel.

Eyeballed

When sun-bathing insects catch the sun's rays, they risk attracting the interest of the stocky, short-legged zebra spider, a spider no bigger than your little fingernail. It is a jumping spider — one of those wickedly effective hunters that specialize in stalking and then jumping on their prey. A jumping spider can leap up to twenty times its own body length and land smack on target, thanks to its excellent eyesight.

You only need to look at a jumping spider to realize how well it can see. It gazes straight back at you with four big eyes that look like car headlights. The outer pair of eyes are sensitive to movement. When they see you, the spider turns around to fix you with the much bigger, inner pair of eyes, which work like binoculars. You can't help wondering what it is thinking.

This tropical jumping spider from the Philippines is one of more than four thousand jumping spider species.

Living Jewels

Some of the creatures that settle on walls are exquisite. Take the cuckoo wasps. These fast-flying, heat-loving insects blaze with metallic greens, blues, and reds, as if cut by a master jeweller. When they get warm, they fly off to find pollen, so you may see them glinting among flowers.

Scuttling Scorpions

Peek behind the flaking plaster of an old garden wall in Mediterranean countries, and you may come face to face with a little black scorpion. Be careful! It may be small, but it has a nasty sting in its tail and will wave its sting and lobster claws in warning.

Scorpions are related to spiders, but they carry poison in their tails, not their fangs. Most of the time, a scorpion does not bother to sting its prey because it can kill insects with its pincers. The sting comes in useful if it is attacked by a bigger animal — including you!

BUG ALERT!

What Lives in the Vegetable Patch?

Nothing beats the taste of home-grown vegetables. You may not agree, but that is certainly the opinion of a whole army of hungry aphids, caterpillars, slugs, and other pests that swarm all over the vegetable patch. Planting so many juicy meals close together makes it particularly easy for the bugs who live there, and the more they eat, the faster they breed.

Many gardeners scatter pesticides that can kill birds and mammals, as well as pests, and that probably are not good for humans, either. If there is no poison around, however, the pests are often attacked by other creatures. The resulting battles can be interesting to watch, so look closely. It's a war zone out there!

Voracious Predators

Aphids make tasty prey for predatory insects. The hungry young of ladybugs, lacewings, and hoverflies fall upon aphids like starving wolves. Each insect devours more than twenty aphids per day. The adult ladybugs and lacewings join the feast and, just like the pests, the more they eat, the faster they breed. Before long, the aphid swarms are almost wiped out, and the ladybugs and their allies have to try their luck elsewhere.

An aphid makes a juicy meal for this ladybug.

Aphid Plagues

Some of the most annoying pests are also among the smallest —tiny aphids, such as greenfly and blackfly. The many different kinds of aphid all live on the sugary sap of plants. They group together on a tender green stem, stab their tubular beaks into its veins, and suck. They can carry virus diseases in their saliva. These infections can turn a healthy green plant into a yellowing, blotchy mess, so aphids are a big problem.

A Taste of Honey

The sap that aphids feed upon is mostly sugary water with a little protein. Aphids need protein to grow, so they have to eat a lot of sap to get enough protein. Eating so much sap means swallowing far more sugar than they need. They get rid of the surplus sugar by squirting it out of their back ends as honeydew. Ants love honeydew and, being ants, they are very well organized, so they have become honeydew farmers.

Black garden ants herd the aphids and "milk" them for honeydew. They defend the aphids from predators, round them up, and herd them into specially made shelters where they are protected from enemies. Most amazing of all, the ants gather aphid eggs in late summer and carry them back to their nest, where the eggs stay safe until they hatch in spring.

Sweet, sugary plant sap is food and drink to this hungry young rose aphid.

Production Line

Aphids multiply rapidly. At the end of summer, male and female aphids mate and produce frost-proof winter eggs. In spring the eggs hatch, but all the young aphids are females who can give birth to their young without mating first. When they find a good food source, each female gives birth to several young every day.

All these young are female, too, and produce their own young within about two weeks. Soon the garden is overrun. Then, as summer fades, a generation of males is born. These mate with females to produce winter eggs, and the cycle starts over again.

Springbugs

Sometimes you will find cabbages or other plants peppered with holes. Look closer, and you may see tiny, shiny flea beetles. The reason for their name soon becomes obvious because, as you approach, they leap in all directions like fleas. They hide until you go away and then sneak back to their meal.

Criminal Damage

Ladybugs are good news in the garden, but a similar beetle is one of the most notorious insect pests of all. The Colorado beetle is a little yellow and black striped beetle first discovered in Colorado in 1824. It was feeding on the leaves of buffalo burr, a wild relative of the potato plant, until farmers settled on the land and started planting potatoes. The beetles discovered a new food, and fifty years later, they had eaten their way right across the United States, stripping potato plants of every leaf. They are so destructive that, in some countries, you should inform the police if you see one!

BUG ALERT!

The Colorado beetle (and larva) comes from the wild, wild West.

Is it edible? A great grey slug investigates a possible meal.

Slugs 'n' Snails

If you visit the vegetable patch on a wet night, you can hear a steady, low munching. Shine your flashlight and you will see slugs and snails, ploughing their way through leaves and tender stems, leaving silvery trails as evidence of their crimes. Gardeners hate them because they can wipe out whole crops in one night. Snails in the garden can be very discouraging.

Most animals do not eat plant stems and leaves because they have trouble digesting the cellulose fibre they are made of. This tough, woody material is actually made of sugar, but the sugar is bound together in such a way that normal digestive juices cannot get at it. Slugs and snails are unusual because they can turn cellulose into sugar. For a slug, a green leaf is as sweet as a peach.

Gas Attack

Cabbages attract all sorts of insects. The most obvious are the caterpillars of the white butterflies that flutter around the cabbage crop all summer. The butterflies lay so many eggs on the cabbages that the teeming caterpillars reduce the vegetables to skeletons.

While they feed, the butterfly caterpillars absorb the mustard oils from cabbage leaves and condense them into a nasty-smelling poison. It is the same stuff as the mustard gas used as a weapon during World War 1. Not surprisingly, birds leave them alone.

What Burrows through the Soil?

It may be dirt to you, but to many small animals, the soil is home. They can find plenty to eat there, provided it is rich in the decaying remains of plants and animals. Microscopic organisms, like fungi and bacteria, feed on these remains and turn them into vital chemicals that plants absorb through their roots. Earthworms find many things to eat in fertile soil. Moles and foxes eat the worms, and, of course, so do early birds.

Earthworms just can't eat enough dirt. They love it!

Wonderworms

Some soils are sweet, crumbly, and fertile, almost entirely due to earthworms. These boneless, blind, slimy creatures spend their lives burrowing through the soil and eating it. They crunch it up in their muscular gizzards, digest the edible fragments, and eject the rest. You will sometimes see their coiled droppings on the surface. Earthworms move mountains of soil every day, churning it up, bringing plant foods to the surface, and allowing air in through their tunnels. Without worms, the soil becomes airless, stale, and dead.

Earthworm Extras
- On wet nights, earthworms emerge from their tunnels to mate and look for food. They keep their tails in their holes so they can retreat from their enemies.
- Australia and southern Africa have monster earthworms more than 10 feet (3 meters) long.
- Anything left on the ground long enough is buried by soil that is brought to the surface by earthworms.

Wormkillers

Earthworms have many enemies — birds, badgers, and foxes snap them up with relish – but the soil itself hides more sneaky killers. They include the shelled slug, Testacella, which feeds on earthworms and other slugs, harpooning them with its barbed tongue.

Another worm killer is the New Zealand flatworm, a fierce, hungry creature that arrives in many parts of the world in potted plants. These flatworms can wipe out whole populations of earthworms, with disastrous results for the soil.

Cluster flies, furry relatives of the housefly, lay eggs on earthworms. When the fly maggots hatch, they eat the worms alive.

Gravedigger

If a cat kills a mouse in the garden, the corpse soon disappears. A bird looking for a meal may eat it, or it may be buried by the extraordinary sexton beetle.

These beetles bury small, dead animals as food for their young. Together, the male and female dig away beneath a body so it sinks into the soil. They skin it and fold it into a tight ball, and then the female lays her eggs. Five days later, the beetle grubs hatch, and their mother helps feed them. Soon, the grubs have eaten the whole mouse and are ready to turn into adults themselves.

Underground Acrobats

A spadeful of soil usually contains wriggling, multi-legged centipedes. Centipedes that live in the soil have amazingly flexible, armored bodies. If a centipede arrives at a dead end in a soil cavity, it just doubles back and crawls out, passing the rest of its long body that is still coming in. Centipedes are hunters, killing insects, spiders, and worms with their poison fangs.

Sexton beetles really like to eat out, dining on the insides of small, dead animals.

What Lives in the Pond?

Nothing attracts wildlife like a pond. Natural ponds teem with life, and even a brand new, man-made pond attracts all kinds of creatures. Add a few water plants and rocks for the animals to hide among, and you have an instant nature reserve. Don't fill the pond with fish, however, because fish eat everything, but you will be amazed by what else moves in.

The most obvious tenants are frogs. In early spring, they gather in force, leaving frogspawn that hatches into tadpoles. Some of the tadpoles may be eaten by ferocious young dragonfly nymphs that live for a year or more at the bottom of the pond. The pond surface provides a hunting ground for several insects that can walk on the water without sinking. It is fascinating to watch, but don't fall in.

This emperor dragonfly has just emerged from its nymph skin.

Air Strike

The most spectacular visitors to a garden pond arrive by air — glittering, brightly colored dragonflies. The bigger ones zoom towards you like helicopters, but they have huge eyes and excellent vision, and they always swerve to avoid you. Insects are not so lucky. Dragonflies are ferocious killers. They snatch their victims out of the air and carry them to a perch to eat.

There are two main types of dragonfly. The big, fast ones settle with their wings outspread. Smaller, fluttery ones, called damselflies, fold their wings along their bodies. Damselflies look delicate, but they are good hunters, too.

34

Killer Nymphs

Female dragonflies lay their eggs in water. Some females just scatter eggs from the air. Others lay them carefully on pondweed. They must mate first, however, and you can often see them sitting on leaves, locked in their heart-shaped mating embrace. Some fly as partners, and the female lays her eggs with the male clinging to her neck with his tail.

The eggs hatch as dull, wingless nymphs that live underwater. They have long legs, good eyesight, and murderously efficient, extendable jaws. Creeping slowly across the bottom of the pond, a nymph stalks a tadpole or similar victim and suddenly shoots out its jaws and grabs its prey. It happens faster than the eye can see, certainly too fast for the unlucky tadpole.

Dragonflies have never breathed fire, but they look like they might!

Magical Transformation

A dragonfly nymph is a nasty, creepy creature, but it magically transforms into an adult dragonfly. It crawls out of the water and clings to a plant stem. After a while, its skin splits, and a pale, crumpled, stumpy-looking animal hauls itself out.

At first, this creature does not look at all like a dragonfly, but gradually, it pumps its body and wings up to their full size. As the metallic colors harden in the sun, they start to glow. Eventually, hours after the dull nymph first emerges, the glittering dragonfly soars up and away, leaving its old, empty self clinging to the stem.

Dragon Facts
- Dragonflies are among the most ancient of flying insects. Fossil remains of huge dragonflies with wingspans of up to $2\frac{1}{2}$ feet (75 cm) have been found in rocks formed more than 300 million years ago — before dinosaurs existed!
- Dragonflies are among the fastest insects, able to fly at speeds of up to 35 miles (56 km) per hour.
- Each eye of a big dragonfly contains up to 30,000 lenses, and it has virtually all-around vision.

Portable Palaces

At the bottom of the pond, you may see creatures that look like tiny stone walls walking about. They are caddis fly larvae, and they build themselves protective cases from pieces of stone, or leaf, or anything they can find in the pond. They glue the pieces together and live inside these homemade shells until they are ready to turn into adults. Pet caddis larvae can be persuaded to use miniature shells, pieces of colored glass, or even precious stones, with dazzling results.

Aqualung

If you're lucky, your garden pond may attract a water spider. This amazing creature lives entirely underwater, but like all spiders, it has to breathe air. It survives by carrying its own air supply in a silvery bubble around its body, like the original aqualung.

It even stores air underwater by trapping air bubbles in bell-shaped webs attached to water weed. The spider uses these diving bells as places to go when it wants to feed, and the female raises her babies in them.

Water spiders carry their own scuba diving gear.

36

Water Tigers

The great diving beetle uses an aqualung technique like the water spider's. This beetle chases prey as large as small fish, driving itself through the water with its paddlelike back legs. It carries an air supply under its hinged wing case, returning to the surface to refill it.

Diving beetle larvae are known as water tigers. They seize their victims with their huge, curved fangs and inject powerful digestive fluids. These fluids turn their victim's insides into slush, which they then suck up through their fangs. Delicious!

The great diving beetle looks for its next fish dinner.

Walking on the Water

To us, the surface of a pond is something you fall through, but to many small insects it is a home. The molecules of water at the surface cling together to form an elastic film called surface tension, which is strong enough to support insects if their feet have special water-resistant pads.

These water walkers include the pond skater, a slender bug that attacks flying insects that crash-land in the water. Attracted by the ripples, it stabs the struggling insects and sucks them dry.

The little water boatman looks like a backswimmer, but it prefers life the right way up.

Bugs A-Plenty

One of the strangest hunters in the pond is the backswimmer. This unusual little bug spends its life swimming on its back or hanging upside down beneath the surface film, watching for prey. When it sees a likely victim, it dives in pursuit, rowing itself along with its long back legs. Then it stabs its prey. It can stab you, too, so watch out!

Predatory bugs are particularly good at living on or in the water. Another one is the ferocious water scorpion. This bug grabs victims with its front legs like an aquatic praying mantis. It breathes air through a long snorkel tube extending from its tail. The tube may look like a sting, but it is the other end you have to avoid!

What Hides in the Woodpile?

A stack of firewood or pile of rocks can make a perfect home for a small creature. The spaces between the logs or stones are sheltered and dry, like natural rock crevices or hollow trees. As long as a stack is not disturbed, many animals can spend their whole adult lives in it.

Some animals live in timber or under bark. Many insect grubs tunnel through the wood of growing or dead trees, and when the timber is sawed up and put in a stack, they continue feeding inside the logs. Eventually, they may hatch as adult beetles, moths, or wasps, but many never get the chance. Even if they emerge, they are likely to be pounced upon by lurking spiders, centipedes, or scorpions. Some of these hunters can be deadly to people, too, so if you're looking in a woodpile, be *very* careful!

Bark beetle galleries make nice patterns, but may destroy the tree.

Tree Killers

If the bark falls off an old log, you may see the galleries, or traces, of bark beetle grubs. The adult beetles lay their eggs under the bark, and when the eggs hatch, the tiny grubs start eating their way out. As they eat, they grow, so their burrows get wider, too. Eventually they turn into beetles and gnaw their way out.

Bark beetle grubs can eat wood because they carry a fungus that digests wood fiber. This fungus causes Dutch elm disease, which has destroyed huge numbers of elm trees in Europe and North America. So if the logs in your woodpile are cut from dead elms, you may see signs of bark beetles.

Wood Processor

The grubs of wood wasps and longhorn beetles do not just burrow under bark. They bore through timber. Like bark beetles, they may carry fungi that make wood digestible, but they also have strong gnawing jaws.

They live for years in the timber and then emerge from large holes as winged adults. Some of these are impressive beasts. Female wood wasps, in particular, have long egg-laying tubes — ovipositors — for drilling into timber. They look like wickedly powerful stings, but they are harmless.

Airborne

An old log makes a snug hiding place for the click beetle, which plays dead by lying on its back when it is threatened. If its predator does not go away, the click beetle bends its head and thorax to form an arch and then suddenly straightens out with a loud click and shoots into the air. Wheee!

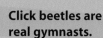

Click beetles are real gymnasts.

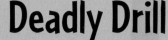

The bionic drill of the ichneumon wasp is tipped with metal for maximum bite.

Deadly Drill

You would think that an insect grub burrowing through solid timber would be safe from attack by other insects, but it is not. The delicate-looking ichneumon wasp is looking for a place to lay her eggs. She has a long, slender ovipositor, with a sharp drill tip that is hardened with metals such as manganese and zinc. She drills her way into a tunnel where a grub is living. Then she lays an egg and flies off.

When the egg hatches, the ichneumon larva latches on to the burrowing grub and starts eating it alive. Meanwhile the grub keeps eating, changing wood into flesh to feed the ichneumon. This is a thankless task since the ichneumon larva kills the grub anyway.

Chink in the Armor

The most numerous creatures in the woodpile are probably wood lice, feeding on rotting wood. These small, armored creatures are crustaceans, like shrimps, crabs, and lobsters. Most crustaceans live in water and breathe through gills, but the wood louse manages to survive on land by carrying a supply of water around in its damp gills. If it dries out, it dies from lack of oxygen, so it always hides in damp places.

Wood lice are often attacked and eaten by centipedes, which stab them with their curved poison fangs. Their main enemy, however, is a six-eyed spider with brick-red legs that has made wood louse-killing its profession. Equipped with extra-long fangs like curved needles, the wood louse spider pierces its victim's back with one fang and pierces its belly with the other. It injects a deadly shot of venom, and the wood louse is history.

Wood lice are relatives of crabs.

Probably the most dangerous spider in the world — the Sydney funnel-web.

BUG ALERT!

Pickaxe Fangs

In southeastern Australia, something very nasty could hide in a log pile. The Sydney funnel-web spider is one of the world's most poisonous spiders. Big, black, and shiny, with huge pickaxe fangs, it usually hides in a silken tunnel that flares out into a funnel-shaped sheet of threads. These work like trip-wires so that when an animal snags its foot on a wire, the spider rushes out, grabs its victim, and stabs it. As the poison gets to work, the spider drags its prey back into its lair and eats it.

The biggest, nastiest-looking funnel-webs are female, but for some reason, the male's venom is much more dangerous, containing nerve poisons that can kill a human within a few hours. Males are also much more likely to wander away from their burrows than females. They may even turn up inside a house. This is one time that being scared of spiders is sensible!

Red for Danger

If you live outside Australia, there's no need to worry about funnel-web spiders. Don't relax just yet, however. The black widow is another deadly spider that lives in many warm countries and often hides in wood piles.

As its name suggests, it is the female that does the damage. She has small fangs, but even they are long enough and strong enough to pierce your skin and inject an awesomely powerful nerve poison, fifteen times stronger than rattlesnake venom. The spider produces it in tiny quantities, but the venom from just one black widow is enough to kill a horse.

Easily distinguished by a bright red mark, black widows are shy, retiring creatures. If they are disturbed, they usually run away and hide. Sometimes they have to defend themselves, however, and if you are in the way and get bitten, you'd better find a doctor — quick!

The black widow spider — the female of the species is definitely the most dangerous.

The black widow is one critter you do not want to upset.

Widow Bytes

- Black widow spiders live all over the world, but the American black widow is probably the most dangerous.
- Male black widows are tiny creatures, and, although they may be just as poisonous as their sisters, they are not big enough to bite you.
- In the days when houses had outdoor toilets, black widow spiders were notorious for lurking there and biting anyone who disturbed them. Nasty!
- The nerve poison of a black widow causes muscle spasms that can paralyze your lungs, with deadly results. If you can manage to keep breathing, you may survive the bite.

What Lives in the Compost Heap?

Many gardens have compost heaps — piles of uprooted weeds, soft green leaves, vegetable peelings, and grass clippings. Over time, this mixture rots down into rich crumbly compost — the best fertilizer of all.

A compost heap teems with microscopic life. Millions of tiny organisms are hard at work, attacking the greenery. They generate heat, and the whole heap warms up. It becomes an ideal nursery for reptiles like the slow worm, a legless lizard that bears beautiful, copper-colored live young. Plenty of slugs and insects inhabit a compost heap for the slow worm to eat, and given the chance, it will live in the heap all year round.

Yellow Peril

One of the most important animals in the compost heap is the dark red, orange-banded brandling worm. It eats dead plant material and turns it into something useful. If you disturb it, however, this worm produces a vile-smelling yellow fluid. Eeuuch!

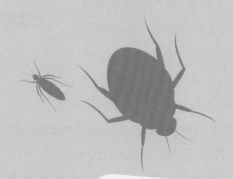

Compost heaps are often alive with juicy worms.

42

Legwaves

Some animals feasting in the compost heap look like shiny black worms, but you will see they have legs — a lot of legs. These are millipedes.

The word millipede means one thousand feet, which is an overstatement, but most have more than one hundred. A millipede's body usually has sixty cylindrical segments, most of which carry two pairs of legs. That makes a total of more than two hundred legs.

A millipede moves its legs one after the other, so the whole row of legs ripples in a wave. The wave drives it along, and all those tiny leg muscles allow it to force its way through stiff soil. Since it dries up quickly in the sun, a millipede soon slips out of sight.

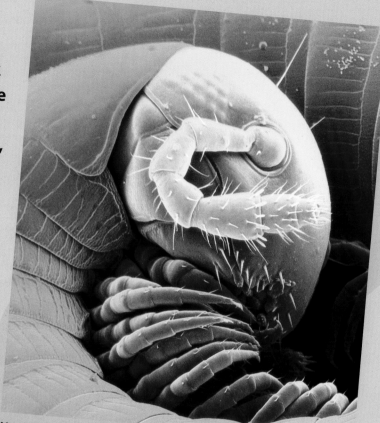

How many legs? A black garden millipede certainly would not be able to afford shoes!

Mighty Mollusc

A compost heap is a feast for large black slugs. These mighty molluscs prefer to eat dead, rotting plants, so they are a lot less destructive than smaller garden slugs.

Obviously, a slug cannot retreat into its shell like a snail, but if you upset one of these big slugs, it pulls in its tentacles and contracts its whole body into a hard, round, prunelike lump.

Springloaded

The smallest creatures that you'll see in the compost heap are springtails. These tiny gray or brown insects feed on rotting vegetation. Each springtail has a long springy fork hinged to its back end. The springtail normally holds this fork tucked under its body, but if it is scared, it releases it. The spring flicks down against the ground, throwing the springtail into the air and, with luck, out of trouble.

Slugs are just snails without shells, but they do pretty well without them.

Quiz Pages

Baffling Bugs

These pictures all show bits of bugs.
Can you name the bugs?

Animal Anagrams

Try unscrambling these jumbled up words to find out
what bugs and microbes are lurking on this page.

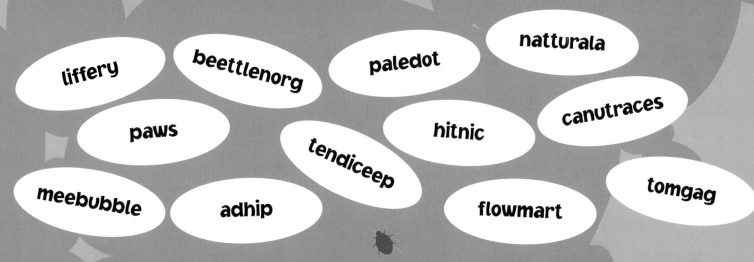

liffery

beettlenorg

paledot

natturala

paws

hitnic

canutraces

tendiceep

meebubble

adhip

flowmart

tomgag

Having a bit of trouble? Are the answers bugging you? See page 46 for some help.

Minibeast Mindbenders

Can you name a creature that:

1   eats dead wood for lunch
2   has an air-supply bubble for breathing in water
3   is a small crustacean whose main enemy is a six-eyed spider
4   can grow to 13 inches (33 cm) long
5   turns its dinner into a milkshake with paralyzing nerve poison
6   has a web no bigger than a postage stamp
7   has a scissor jaw and sucks blood
8   can turn its head all the way around
9   is small, green, and a relative of the greenfly
10 is a cabbage muncher that makes its own deadly mustard gas

How many did you score?

1-4   Good start! Now go back and do some more reading.
5-7   Great! You have certainly learned a lot.
8+   Excellent! You must be the world's expert on what lives in the grass, on the flowers, and even in the vegetable patch!

Nasty Numbers

Can you remember the answers to these nauseating number puzzles?

1 A swarm of locusts can contain up to how many individual insects?
   a 5,000
   b 50,000
   c 5 million
   d 50 billion

2 How fast can dragon-flies travel?
   a up to 10 mph (16 km/h)
   b up to 16 mph 26 km/h)
   c up to 35 mph (56 km/h)
   d up to 40 mph (65 km/h)

3 How far away can you hear a cricket's "song"?
   a up to 65 feet (20 m)
   b up to 500 yards (457 m)
   c more than 1 mile (2 km)
   d more than 3 miles (4.8 km)

4 How long can monster earthworms grow?
   a 3 feet (1 m)
   b 6 feet (2 m)
   c 10 feet (3 m)
   d 13 feet (4 m)

5 About how many legs does a millipede usually have?
   a more than 100
   b more than 200
   c more than 500
   d more than 1,000

6 What is the legspan of the goliath bird-eating spider?
   a 5 inches (13 cm)
   b 8 inches (20 cm)
   c 11 inches (28 cm)
   d 16 inches (41 cm)

Answers

Nasty Numbers

1 d 2 c
3 c 4 c
5 b 6 c

Minibeast Mindbenders

1 Termite
2 Water spider
3 Wood louse
4 Stick insect
5 Assassin bug
6 Gladiator spider
7 Blackfly
8 Praying mantis
9 Froghopper
10 Cabbage white butterfly caterpillar

Animal Anagrams

maggot

flatworm

aphid

bumblebee

crustacean

chitin

centipede

wasp

tarantula

tadpole

greenbottle

firefly

Baffling Bugs

1 Bee fly
2 Orb web spider
3 Garden spider
4 Ruby-tailed cuckoo wasp
5 Bumblebee
6 Desert locust
7 Black widow spider
8 Tropical jumping spider

46

Index

a

ant, black, 9, 29
  fire, 9
  harvester, 9
  tending aphids, 29
aphid, 4, 28, 29, 30
  blackfly, 29
  greenfly, 29
  mating, 30
Argiope, 23
assassin bug, 22

b

backswimmer, 37
badger, 33
bark, beetle gallery, 38
bat, eaten, 11
bee, African, 14
  bumblebee, 8, 15
  honeybee, 14
  killer, 14
  leaf-cutter, 21
  mining, 8, 13
bee fly, 13
beetle, click, 39
  Colorado, 30
  flea, 30
  galleries, 38
  great diving, 37
  lily, 17
  longhorn, 39
  rose chafer, 16
  sexton, 33
  soldier, 16
bird, 32, 33

blackfly, 5, 19
blackfly aphid, 29
buddleia, 12
bug, assassin, 22, 23
  shield, 22
bumblebee, 8, 15
butterfly, cabbage white, 31
  tortoiseshell, 12

c

caddis fly larvae, 36
caterpillar, 20, 31
cellulose, 31
centipede, 33, 40
chitin, 12
cicada, 22
cricket, bush, 21
  field, 7
  mole, 7
crustaceans, 40
cuckoo spit, 17

d

damselfly, 34
digestion, 5, 8, 31, 32
dragonfly, emperor, 34
  nymph, 35

e

earthworm, 32, 33
earwig, 17
enzyme, 8

f

firefly, 8
flatworm, New Zealand, 33
fly, bee fly, 13
  blackfly, 5, 19
  cluster, 33
  greenbottle, 26
  horsefly, 26
  hoverfly, 18, 28
fossil, dragonfly, 35
fox, 33
frog, eaten, 11
  spawn, 34
  tadpole, 34, 35
froghopper, 17

g

glowworm, 8
grasshopper, 6, 7
  meadow, 7
greenbottle, 26
greenfly, 17, 29

h

habitat, 4, 5, 6
honeybee, 14
honeydew, 29
honeysuckle, 13
horsefly, 26
hoverfly, 18, 28

47